Aspergers,
Our Way of Life:
An Amazing Adventure

Margaret Dillane

ISBN 9780755280032

Contents

Foreword

This book has come to life as a result of spending years looking for something I already had. As a young girl I would spend hours walking along the beach in search of something I thought would give me everlasting happiness, peace and freedom. I wrote poems; read endless books and in the end left my homeland of Ireland in search of the 'happy ever after'.

Needless to say the happy ever after was not found… in the 'Disney sense' of the word, but a greater happiness and peace was to be my gift.

I became a mum and through a journey of postnatal depression, marriage, divorce, Aspergers, epilepsy and self-reflection, I reached a point in my life where being Irish and walking on Cockleshell beach in County Kerry was to be my return and the beginning of this precious book.

As the mother of a child with Aspergers it became clear to me early on that my daughter found it hard to read the social signals that most of us take for granted. She would get very anxious about things that I saw as 'so simple' but to her were a cause of great anxiety and confusion. I was at a loss as to why socialising did not come naturally to her. It was not until she was diagnosed with Aspergers syndrome that it all made sense.

Once I had the diagnosis I set out to discover as much as I could about this condition and observe how it presents itself in my daughter.

Along the way there have been many tears of frustration, confusion and total desperation but the most amazing thing about this wonderful journey are the great lessons, learning and self-discovery that has taken place.

My daughter is amazing and her sense of justice is so heightened that it truly amazes me how she understands life in a way that has been lost in our fast, throwaway world.

Aspergers syndrome is a condition that causes certain difficulties and anxieties when trying to make sense of social situations, but it is also something that brings a deep sensitivity and understanding that many of us have lost in this desensitised world we live in today.

I am writing this book in the hope of bringing awareness to the everyday challenges living with Aspergers brings and in the hope that people will take the time to understand it before making a judgement.

I dedicate this book to all the families and children living every day with Aspergers syndrome. To the wonderful family I call mine and to my precious daughter, who was my reason for taking a deep look at where I have come in my life and how I got here.

Thank you,

Mags

Introduction

> *"Our deepest fear is not that we are inadequate. Our deepest fear is that we are powerful beyond measure. It is our light, not our darkness that most frightens us. We ask ourselves, "Who am I to be brilliant, gorgeous, talented and fabulous?" Actually, who are you not to be? You are a child of God.*
>
> *Your playing small doesn't serve the world. There is nothing enlightened about shrinking so that people won't feel insecure around you. We were born to make manifest the glory of God that is within us. It's not just in some of us; it is in everyone. And as we let our light shine, we unconsciously give other people permission to do the same. As we are liberated from our own fear, our presence automatically liberates others."*
>
> **[Marianne Williamson]**

Liberation from my own fears was to become the biggest part of this amazing journey of Aspergers. I was lost in the many patterns set up in childhood and believed this to be who I was. We cannot avoid these patterns and as a result our fears and anxieties, happiness and joys, all stem from these beliefs, where the majority of us are simply living from the script.

It's funny how for years we live in the shadow of our

pattern and conditioning, in the hope that one day in the 'future' we will be the person we were born to be.

However, that future time never seems to come because we are so lost in the prison of who we think we are that we are afraid to take a step out into the unknown and dare to be who we truly are.

We get lost, not only in our own patterns, but in the patterns and expectations of others and as a result keep ourselves exactly where we are – afraid to move out of the comfort of our conditioned self and find the freedom in our own truth.

I found myself pondering this very fact for years and as a result found myself reading endless books from Louise Hay to Eckhart Tolle. I immersed myself in the words of others hoping to find all the answers to my life, oblivious to the fact that all the answers were to be found in me, by me, with the help of the universe, in the form of the turmoil and struggles that became my natural teachers. I was searching for ways to transgress my outer limitations and go beyond what I perceived as the conditioned truth, my conditioned and confused self. I was looking for ways to transform and find a better 'me', but all the time I was getting lost in my perceived expectations of who I should be and my need to please everyone.

I was lost in my own self-made prison and realised that I was doing the same thing to my daughter.

Thankfully my true understanding of my outer limitations became all the more real when I became a mother. My daughter became my greatest teacher and through a process of fear and confusion, I began to awaken to the real me. I began to acknowledge my limitations and see them for what they were; limitations of the body/the conditioned self, and on realising this I was able to begin to tap into the limitlessness of my true self/soul. However, this was not as easy as it sounded. The problem I had was that for years I strove for perfection in everything I did and as a result always fell from my self-made pedestal with a mighty bang.

What was I to do? On one level I knew I had to change, but before I could change I had to accept where I was now. However, accepting where I *was did not come* easy because I fought, struggled and pushed to be anywhere but where I was. It was not until I had tried everything else that I finally had to surrender and accept where I was and it was through this acceptance that I was finally able to see that the person I had become was not the person I was born to be.

As a result, I began to reflect on my interactions with my daughter, which led me to putting pen to paper and sharing my thoughts with whoever happens to find this story interesting… not to worry if you don't, I won't take it personally as I have worked on my fear of failure for 40 years!

Where I Began

"We do not learn from experience… we learn from reflecting on experience."

John Dewey

It all began with my desire to be a mum. My dream was always to be a mother; I longed to have my own child and my dream came true when I was 38 years old. I was sure that having my little girl was all I needed to be happy and so I was ready to live my life with a 'happy ever after'.

However, that was not to be the case. I got postnatal

depression and suddenly my dream and my reality of motherhood were very different. I was caught in a straightjacket of my desire to be a mum and my reality of having postnatal depression.

I was lost in a very dark place, unable to feel the love I knew was shut up inside me. My darling little girl was so vulnerable because she was unable to understand what was happening to me and I was unable to understand what was happening to her. I knew she needed the other side of me but I was unable to be 'me'. I did not recognise myself as I could not understand why I was feeling so low.

The irony of all this was that I was so happy when I found out I was pregnant and spent the whole nine months in love with my unborn child. I was certain that being a mum was all I wanted, so having these strange, unnatural feelings felt so confusing.

This was so alien to me, as I saw myself as always being in control and a 'go-getter', I was always looking for the next challenge, the next problem to solve. I always lived my life in the fast lane and at the age of 19 I left my home in Ireland in search of adventure and fun and to find my life's purpose. I travelled to America to work for a couple of years, returned to live in London and studied to be a Montessori teacher. At the age of 30+ I decided to go back to university to study for my degree and then to continue to do my master's degree. I was always on top of things, controlling all aspects of my life, yet here I was at the age of 38 unable to deal with motherhood. What had happened to me? How had I lost my way? How did I reach this place in my life?

I always wanted to be a mother and I knew that somewhere deep inside me what was happening to me was not 'me', but I just could not stop it from happening; so I knew the only thing I could do was to accept it and get on with it.

I had to do the best I could to live with postnatal depression for whatever duration I had to.

And that is exactly what I did; I was like a robot, I did things robotically – woke up, cooked, cleaned, took care of Yasmin and tried to sleep at night without worrying, which was impossible because worry and fear are the best friends of depression so I had no choice but to live with them for the duration. I woke up each day only to repeat the cycle of worry, fear and anxiety all over again. I remember thinking that this did not feel right. Surely there must be something wrong, because I knew deep inside of me that I was ready to be a mum. I had longed for years to be a mum and never for one moment thought about depression. I had heard of postnatal depression but assumed that it happened to other women and not to me. The irony of all this was that I had worked with children for years as a Montessori teacher and thought that my experience of working with children would allow me to be a natural mother. How wrong I was! Although I was ready for motherhood, the one thing I had not put into the equation was that life as I knew it would change and change drastically, which was certainly a contributing factor to my depression.

I wanted things to remain the same and as a result of this wanting I had not prepared myself emotionally for the changes that motherhood would bring.

I had organised all the outer changes, from buying a cot to getting the clothes, to packing my bag for the hospital, but I had not prepared myself emotionally. I did not think there was a need to do that because I was so happy being pregnant. So here I was at the age of 38, a mother with postnatal depression, trying to make sense of something that seemed alien to me.

And so life continued with me trying to live with depression, knowing somewhere deep inside me that one day by the grace of God I would come out of the slumber of postnatal depression and find my way back to life, and I did; it was like waking from a terrible nightmare. It was like breathing for the first time and seeing for the first time. I wanted to experience and enjoy every moment of being Yasmin's mum. I wanted to sing from the rooftops and dance in the street. I wanted the world to know that I was a happy mum.

However, instead of shouting from the rooftops I decided to write a poem for Yasmin, so that when she was old enough it would somehow explain the loss I felt in having postnatal depression and my longing to be free to love her. I read it to her recently and she loved it, so I decided to include it in this book.

Yasmin

My little girl I lost my way
when you came into my life,

I got postnatal depression
and life was difficult as a wife.

I never knew how to show you love
or protect you from all my pain,

I lost my way and lived with fear
and inside my heart was rain.

I looked at you so many times
and begged of God above

To allow me to feel the truth inside
my heart so full of love.

I asked Him every day
when you were first born

To take away the pain
the loss, the feeling of forlorn.

I prayed that He would show me
the meaning of my life,

8

But all the time I tried so hard
The pain would cut me like a knife.

And then I knew with the help of God
That one day I would be well

And tell you how much I loved you
and get out of my living hell.

And so today my precious child
I fight within myself

To give the best of mummy
And put the old one on the shelf.

And now I know I had to experience
the feelings of depression

In order to see the love I have
to share with my little precious.

My precious little angel,
my Yasmin, my little love.

The little girl who came to me
and fits me like a glove.

My little girl; I love you so
And want to help you be

The precious little person
Who has made a change in me.

The wonderful thing about life is that it keeps going and stops for no one or nothing. And so with the passing of time I began to reflect on how I was living my life. I realised that I spent my days rushing and running around to get things done so that I could tick them off my endless list of things to do, so that one day I would find the peace and love I was searching for. I found myself constantly doing with very little time for 'being'. My world had become a place where the pace of life had become faster. I was in a rush to compete, get things done and live in the fast lane. It seemed the more I could fit into my day, the more accomplished I would feel.

Ironically I was still left with a sense of emptiness or loss that nothing seemed to be able to fill. Life had somehow become a chore, where very little time was given to the 'present moment' and very little understanding was given to things that didn't fit the norm. This was to become a recurring theme in my life as being 'normal' was something I was forever striving to be, to the detriment of my true self.

I had first-hand experience of the fear of not being normal when my daughter was diagnosed with Aspergers syndrome. It became apparent to me that there was very little understanding of this condition and people who were not aware were not very understanding. However, I realised it was not only 'other' people who were intolerant, as I too was also unaware and had very little understanding of this condition. This was a guiding factor in how I lived with my daughter. As I was striving for normality and the need to have everything 'right' my little girl was striving to be herself. I was in fact causing her a lot of unnecessary anxiety and pain because all she wanted was to be herself.

Therefore, in order to be of any help to my daughter, I embarked on a journey of self-discovery and began by looking at myself and my perceptions and prejudices. And so I became what I like to call a 'reflective mum'... However, what began to unravel before me was not what I had expected.

I realised that life had become a list of things to do... I got up in the morning, went to work, planned my day, worked for hours, came home, cooked, ate, tidied up, slept and began it all over again the next day. I moved up and down in prayer, sometimes connecting, sometimes not. I was simply running to get to the next thing in my life without being part of the process. I was running to get 'somewhere', but I did not know where this 'somewhere' was.

I found myself wondering if this was all there was to life, was this 'the true purpose of life'; was this 'my purpose'? Surely there must be more. Was I living in a trance waiting for the great moment when I would be inspired to take a leap, a jump, a journey to the unknown? But one day I'd wake up and I'd be half a century. Where would the time have gone? When was this great moment going to happen? When am I going to understand? I asked myself – what am I waiting for? I didn't know, but somewhere deep inside something was telling me that it was amazing. How would I find it? I knew I had to take a chance and begin a journey of self-discovery, even though I knew that I would uncover things I would not want to see.

But before I could begin this journey, the first thing I had to do was to get my head around the fact that my daughter had a diagnosis of Asperger syndrome and so I started an endless search for as much information as I could to help me understand this diagnosis.

It was at this time that I had a meeting with the psychologist who had made the diagnosis. I presumed the meeting was about the diagnosis and about understanding Aspergers.

However, I was in for a surprise, she had called the meeting to talk to me about 'me'... She began to explain to me that my rushing, obsessive, overactive, over talking, hyperactive, controlling, perfectionist, organised personality was not helping Yasmin's condition. WOW! Bombshell! What could this lady be talking about...? All the things she had listed had helped me to keep going and stay in control. And here she was telling me that this was causing more confusion for Yasmin and as a result I was in fact igniting her anxiety.

How was I going to stop being who I had grown to become? I knew I was loud and talked too much. I knew I was passionate and overemotional. I knew I was weird because I had been told it enough times, but all I could think was, "This is who I am."

After all, I'm Irish and the one thing we know how to do well is talk, be passionate, and in many cases, be a little weird.

And so I was faced with a decision, Yasmin needed a calm, relaxed, peaceful, not too talkative, anxious-free mum. Not too much to ask – are you kidding? This was all I knew... I had become this person, I had mastered this hyperactive, overanxious, manic control freak over many years and here was this lady who had just met me a few times telling me exactly what I did not want to hear. How could I change what I had learnt to become; the thing I had relied on for so many years to get me through each stage of my life?

I was now faced with a dilemma; on the one hand I knew that Yasmin needed and deserved better and on the other hand, how was I to change who I had become?

The one thing I knew for sure was that I had no control over her diagnosis, but I did have some control over myself. But how was I going to change what I'd spent the whole of my life perfecting?

And so the next phase of my journey began. I had to take a deeper look at me and expose the part of me that was causing her unnecessary pain, confusion and anxiety.

I once read that in order to take this leap, this journey, this next step, we need to be equipped with the right tools.

> *"A traveller needs appropriate maps, the means for travelling, for example a vehicle, fuel and provisions. He also needs a wider understanding of the terrain and environment of the journey."*
>
> **[Shaykh Fadhlalla, ASK]**

It was then I knew that I had to get to know my terrain and equip myself with the right tools for the journey and so the journey from Aspergers to understanding began. However, there was another variable to add to this equation; not only was my daughter dealing with

13

Aspergers she was also living with epilepsy. And therefore I had to ensure that I was well informed on how these two conditions not only exhibited in my daughter, but how I could best support her in her understanding of both Aspergers and epilepsy.

The road has not been an easy one and certainly not one that you can find an easy map to follow, but my gratitude and deepest love are extended to God for helping me find my way in this rough terrain, to my family for their amazing support and love, to my beautiful friends who are there when I want to shout and to my precious daughter who shone the light for me to follow.

And so I began to search for the maps that would lead me to some kind of understanding of this condition called Aspergers, a condition I knew very little about other than to be known as a social communication condition.

As a Montessori teacher I felt a deep desire to look at this condition from a holistic viewpoint and therefore began with what I knew best… the Montessori philosophy.

My Need to Understand

It is rather ironic that I became a Montessori teacher in the 80s, as back then I had not realised that I would one day use this philosophy in trying to gain an understanding of my beautiful daughter and her diagnosis of Aspergers.

Ironically Dr Montessori found this method of educating children by observing children with special needs and realised that children with special needs had a great ability to learn given the correct environment. She believed that the environment and the adult were of paramount importance in assisting the child's natural development; something that became my main focus in helping my daughter, as both her environment and the adults around her were the main causes for her meltdowns and anxieties.

Montessori believed that all children have within them an absorbent mind that allows them to absorb their environment in a way that allows learning to happen automatically. However, for children with Aspergers it is not as easy, as they have to deal with the many sensory issues relating to their diagnosis. Therefore understanding this condition is of major importance if the adult is to be a gateway for the child.

I agree that the importance of understanding the absorbent mind is crucial, but more importantly the role of the adult in the child's environment is of greater importance. Montessori believed that the role of the adult must be one of awareness and understanding, thus witnessing the development of the human soul.

> "We teachers can only help the work going on as servants wait upon a master. We then become witnesses to the development of the human soul; the emergence of the new man who will no longer be the victim of events but thanks to his clarity of vision will become able to direct and mould the future of mankind."
>
> **[Maria Montessori]**

I knew that I did not want my daughter to become a victim of events, as I knew that she had so much to offer in the moulding of not only her future, but the future of mankind.

But this could only be achieved with the assistance of a conscious adult and once again I knew that this had to begin with me. I had to wake up and become conscious. However, the million-dollar question was... how was I going to achieve this task?

I began to think that I was expecting too much of myself and at times I would fall off the wagon and resort to childlike behaviour – kicking and screaming in the hope that I did not have to take responsibility for myself, willing my fairy godmother to wave her magic wand and make everything OK.

I had learnt in my teacher training that it was the duty

of the adult to become inwardly conscious, to awaken to the inner truth and therefore to prepare herself for the task of assisting the child in his/her development, as a servant prepares to serve a master. I remember reading this when I was a young student of 20 and remembering being rather surprised to think of myself as a servant, surely as an adult I was the guardian of the child and not the servant of the child? It was not until many years of learning and missed opportunities that I came to realise that Montessori was very apt in comparing the work of the teacher to that of a servant. Years later I learnt that the key ingredient in the ability to serve is 'humility', something I did not understand as a young trainee teacher. It has taken many years of mistakes to realise and understand the importance of 'humility' and its place in the development of the child.

Humility is a crucial ingredient in life and so with this in mind I set out to look at myself and my understanding of humility as the mother of a child with Aspergers.

The irony of all this was that while I was well versed in Dr Montessori's philosophy and the importance of the adult's preparation in working with the child, I was not internalising her philosophy and using it as the transformative tool it is. Dr Montessori did not only believe in the preparation of the adult, she also believed that the adult must be willing to reflect on her practice with the child. She believed that the adult must not look at the child as a teacher looks at a pupil, only conscious of filling their heads with knowledge, but she must be so brave as to see the child that is not yet there… The adult, according to Dr Montessori:

> *"...must have a kind of faith that the child will reveal himself through work."*

I realised that for years I was simply practising her theory with very little awareness of the amazing transformative tool the Montessori philosophy really is.

In my quest for getting everything right I was simply working on the outer stuff – the things I had learnt from a book – and using what I had learnt more as a teaching tool than a transformative tool. Ironically with my daughter I was unable to see the child that was not yet there as I was so busy trying to make her 'normal' and become the child I thought she should be.

I was aware of the brilliance of the Montessori method, but when it came to my own child I resorted to the traditional ways I was taught and found myself filled with expectations of how my child should learn, rather than how she actually learns.

Too often we put ourselves in the position of 'makers' of our children, always trying to get our children to do what we believe is best for them, unaware of the fact that they have an internal agenda that instinctively knows what is right. In turn we end up becoming the child's greatest obstacle.

> *"I am not a teacher but an awakener."*
>
> **[Robert Frost]**

We believe and justify, with a somewhat warped sense

of responsibility, that it is our duty to control our children, imprisoning them in our endless expectations.

> *"The child's parents are not his makers but his guardians. They must protect and care for him in the deepest sense… that goes beyond the interests and ideas of external life… and they must understand that such love is the conscious part of a deeper guidance. It is for parents to visualise and take up the social question facing us at the present day, the struggle to establish the rights of the child in the world."*
>
> **[Maria Montessori: The Secret of Childhood]**

I knew that I had become immersed in Yasmin's outer world, trying to get everything right on an outer level; from learning to ride a bike to learning to read and write. I was lost in her external world, while all the time she was lost in her internal world. She would sit and shake her piece of paper, lost in thoughts and stories of worlds she made up in her head. She was happy to be left alone and get lost in her own world, yet all the time I was trying to get her out of her world as I believed I knew what was best for her.

I was so lost in trying to get her to connect to what I thought was right for her, when all the time she wanted to be allowed to dream and imagine and get lost in her own thinking.

The simple reality is that Yasmin sees the world in her way and I was trying to get her to see the world the way I see it. This was one of the many realisations I had as I was learning first-hand about Aspergers syndrome. I was so lost in the condition of Aspergers, having learnt all about the lack of social understanding and interactions, that I could not see how Yasmin was seeing and interacting with the world. I could see that she found social situations difficult and a reason to feel anxious, but I could not understand why. Being Irish we are big with social interactions and meeting people and being comfortable with people was something I believe I wanted for Yasmin. It was not until I realised that I spent the majority of my life trying to please people, people I did not even know, and here I was trying to make Yasmin do the same thing.

I knew I had to stop and question how I saw Yasmin. I knew I had to stop trying to make her like me and instead honour who she is... my precious gift from God.

"To taste the sweetness of life you must have the power to forget the past"

[Brahma Kumaris]

I was finally beginning to become aware of what she was learning from me and the way I interacted with the world and her. At the time when Yasmin was born I was trying to control everything around me, as I was always fearful of what life would bring and in some warped way I thought if 'I' controlled everything around me I would somehow get it right. However, as a result I found myself more lost than found. It was through the need to control everything that I realised I was unable to sustain the level of control I was striving for. This became another clue in the journey from confusion to clarity and in what I was teaching Yasmin, by my reactions, example and way of life.

Children Learn What They Live

"Let us treat them [the children] *therefore with all the kindness which we would wish to help develop in them."*
Dr Maria Montessori

And so I set about looking at what I was teaching Yasmin through my way of life. So much research has been done recently to show the considerable impact and influence conditioning, environment and upbringing have on the formative years of the child and in the formation of his/ her personality and character. Not that either are carved in stone, but one cannot underestimate the work required to then undo and unlearn the habits and behaviour of early environmental, parental and cultural upbringing.

Nothing can stop the natural development of the child but many things can hinder it… something I was to experience first-hand.

I have spent the last 12 years of my daughter's life wondering how to educate and assist her natural development and along the way I have fallen into many societal, governmental and expectational traps. I bought into the pressures of so-called child experts; listened to endless amounts of advice on how to feed her, bathe her, the correct sleeping, eating and toilet-training positions, all to the detriment of my sanity and self-esteem.

Having postnatal depression and feeling as if I was possessed by some alien being added to my sense of guilt and low self-esteem. I hadn't a clue who I was or what I was doing. I was lost in a very strange world of wanting to be a mother but not knowing how. I later realised that my soul-searching journey began at this point, with my tiny newborn on my hip watching my confusion and struggle unfold before her. If I was lost in the world of depression and pain, how was she feeling? This later became one of the main clues to my understanding of my daughter's Aspergers.

Her early childhood had a major role to play in her interpretation of the world and her place in it. While I was lost in depression, confusion and misunderstanding, she was trying to make sense of a world that made no sense to her and I was not able to help her, as I too was unable to make sense of where I was.

It was at this time that I began to wonder what my

child was learning from my example. I was caught in my own world of confusion and self-pity, looking for ways of finding happiness while all the time my little girl was developing before my eyes. I was very aware of her outer changes and focussed on her education and daily needs, completely oblivious to her inner life and the example she was seeing in the confusion around her. I knew from my Montessori training that learning and development is rooted in relationship and all relationships are dependent on what the child lives with and so I had to begin to focus on what my little girl was living with.

Now anyone who knows me knows that I get totally immersed in the universal law of attraction and I believe that we attract things to us by the way we feel and live. And so when the following poem mysteriously dropped into my inbox I was not surprised as I took it as the lesson I needed at that time. So I will share it with you...

If children live with criticism; they learn to condemn
If children live with hostility; they learn to fight
If children live with ridicule; they learn to be shy
If children live with shame; they learn to feel guilty
If children live with tolerance; they learn to be patient
If children live with encouragement; they learn confidence
If children live with praise; they learn to appreciate
If children live with fairness; they learn justice
If children live with security; they learn faith
If children live with approval; they learn to like themselves
If children live with acceptance and friendship; they learn to find love in the world.

[Dorothy Law Nolte]

Here it was in black and white; our children live with the parts of us they experience. If our children experience 'love', they learn to love. If our children live with fear, they learn to be afraid.

I knew that my daughter was, at some level, experiencing my fear, although I thought I was hiding it from her. I knew that fear was a very damaging expression of who I was, but it had simply become part of my life.

Fear had become something that I lived with on a daily basis. From fear of not having enough to fear of not being enough, I was indirectly teaching my child to be afraid.

I was in fact feeding my child this fear every day when I was comparing her to another child, complaining about the world and all that was happening around us, complaining about my life, blaming her for something she had done or something she had not done; the list was endless. Fear had become second nature to me and had begun to disempower me, leaving me feeling helpless. I had not realised the power of my fears and what my precious little girl was picking up from my fears every day.

> *"We worry about what a child will become tomorrow yet we forget that she is someone today."*
>
> **[Stacia Tauscher]**

Worry and fear were keeping me stuck and stopping me from taking a step forward. I knew at some level, from all my reading, that life is happening in the now; it is not happening in tomorrow or in yesterday. It is happening right here, right now; something our children instinctively know and this is why they simply live in the moment. They are not concerned about what happened yesterday and they are not thinking about tomorrow. This is something we indirectly teach them with our fears and anxieties. Children are simply living in the moment, savouring every aspect of this great life. Children are amazing and can do amazing things, if we can only trust in this amazement and allow it to unfold.

Our children are enough; they do not need us to make them enough or make them into something we believe is good for them… God has done a great job and all we need to do is love them and great things will happen.

Unfortunately, as much I wanted to see it like this, the problem continued because of how and what I believed my child should be and more importantly because of what I believed about myself. I was not happy but I had fooled myself into believing that I was happy. I had simply got used to feeling like this, thinking it was normal. I realised that as soon as I began to put my expectations on my beautiful, perfect daughter I was indirectly telling her that she was 'not enough'.

> *"Children are likely to live up to what you believe of them."*
>
> **[Lady Bird Johnson]**

I was unable to see the beautiful child in front of me, as I was lost in the child I wanted her to become. What kind of madness was this? Up to the age of two years we somehow instinctively know that we must allow our children to guide us in understanding their needs. When they cry we try a variety of things, from food, to sleep, to changing a wet nappy. We have no expectation that they should stop crying until they are ready. When the child is ready to walk we wait for the child to show us. In fact we wait with great joy and announce to the world, "She has taken her first step." It is an amazing moment.

We have not planned it, set a schedule for it, or put it in a timetable. We simply wait for nature to take its course.

However, when the child turns two the training begins… the letters, numbers, colours etc. are all brought out in anticipation of teaching the child.

We are in some kind of hurry to get in as much teaching as we possibly can. Why? It's simple… Fear… Fear that they will not be 'good enough', 'smart enough', 'beautiful enough', 'polite enough', 'kind enough'… the list is endless… And here I was, the mother of a beautiful, precious little girl, a Montessori teacher and the reader of endless books, doing exactly that to my own child because of my fear of the future for my child.

It is ironic that up to the age of two we allow the child's natural development to unfold before us, and unfold it does in a most amazing manner, with no need for formal education. Then at the age of 2-3 the pencil is put in his hand, the numbers are put before him and it's time to learn. What strange happening occurs around this time? Where in the great book of life do we learn that this is the time to push the child to become a man?

Learning is natural and is ongoing from the moment we awake to the moment of sleep.

It is not something we have to do or plan, it is

something that happens. We do not have to interfere with this natural process – all we need to do is to provide an environment conducive to learning, an environment where one size does not fit all, an environment where the uniqueness and individuality of each child is honoured and valued.

This was something I had to learn to do with my daughter as I was still stuck in a time warp of traditional teaching… with the 'you listen and I teach' philosophy.

> *"Education is not the learning of facts, but the training of the mind to think."*
>
> **[Albert Einstein]**

Education: The Greatest Gift or a Difficult Chore?

Our Education System

"Everybody is a genius. But if you judge a fish by its ability to climb a tree, it will live its whole life believing that it is stupid."

- Albert Einstein

Education is one of the greatest gifts we can give our children. It has been called the greatest weapon, the greatest tool. Education awakens the human being to the world in a way that allows great progression to take place.

However, the problem I see today is the way education is given to our children, something I was to experience when my daughter went to school. She was eager to go to school as she had a desire to be with other children. Unfortunately the reality of her school experience added to her sense of social confusion because she was not allowed to express herself in her way, but was being made to fit into what the teachers wanted for her. It felt like they were banging a square peg into a round hole and destroying my daughter in the process.

> *"Autists are the ultimate square pegs and the problem with pounding a square peg into a round hole is not that the hammering is hard work. It's that you're destroying the peg."*
>
> **[Paul Collins]**

With all my experiences of my daughter's schooling I was faced with the incessant need to make her fit into what the school thought she should be. Education, in my experiences, had become a very robotic process, where one size fits all and all children are expected to achieve according to a set of government standards. There is little room for individuality or difference. It has become a chore and something that has to be done if you want to become somebody in life.

Education has been sold as something that is crucial to existence and if you are not educated in the 'school sense' of the word then you are 'stupid' and will not amount to much. This is one thing that every parent fears... fear that their child will be 'stupid' and will not achieve, so they will buy into anything that promises to ensure that their child will perform for the tests and thus fit into the 'norm' at whatever cost to the child.

Ironically, as I write this down, I realise that I too had become programmed and each day when I would collect my daughter from school I would ask her about her day. I was not only concerned about what she learnt but I was also concerned about how she had behaved and what the teachers had said to her.

And each day, without fail, she would tell me that they took her string (a piece of paper she shakes) away from her and she had to sit on a chair for ten minutes. It was insanity because her piece of paper was the one thing that helped her to feel secure, yet here they were taking it from her and banging away at the perfection of my child in order to make her 'fit the norm'. And I was letting this happen because I did not trust my instincts and blood-curdling feelings as she would tell me the same thing each day. I was programmed like everyone else to try to get her to 'fit in'.

How wrong I was...

In fact we have become so programmed that we focus on education and tests as being the answer to society's problems, forgetting the importance of whole development and the understanding of the self.

Education should not be a means to an end but a joy and a privilege; something a child wants to do, not something they have to do. Education must encompass the development of the whole person, not just the intellect.

Unfortunately, in our schools today children do not seem to truly enjoy this amazing learning process, as the love of learning has been taken from them with the heavy workload of subjects. I asked my friend's daughter, who recently started high school, how she was enjoying school. Her response was, "I haven't got detention yet!" Her response made me think and left me with a sense of sadness at the way education is experienced by our future generation. It showed me that her fear of detention was taking precedence over the amazing experiences she could have.

On one level I can understand the push to get things done, but the problem lies in the fact that the curriculum is too heavy; there are too many subjects which in turn changes the whole learning experience from one of joy to one of fear, as the chid is pushing to get everything done in time.

The fact that children sit at desks listening to teachers regurgitate facts that they are asked to record and learn, to later regurgitate for an exam whether they are interested in the subject or not, adds to the apathy that many children may feel.

By the time the child has regurgitated the regurgitated information it has become stale and the love of hearing and experiencing something fresh and new is lost. Now if you have ever been to a bakery first thing in the morning when the bread has just come out of the oven you would never again want to eat anything but freshly baked bread. It smells, tastes, feels and looks so much better.

I believe that this is the same with knowledge. The information resourced and found by the child himself (with some guidance from the teacher) is fresh, alive and tastes delicious. The child is alive in the research and in the process of finding the information that calls to him. The child who is interested wants to learn; he is eager to explore and to find out more. All we have to do is look at a young child of three or four, who is forever seeking out, searching and exploring. He wants to find out as much as he can and is forever asking, "Why?"

He wants to know and will do everything he can to find out. Young children are not satisfied with silly answers, they want to know facts – how things work, where things come from, what makes things move etc.… they are filled with endless questions. And this is exactly how it should be… children want to learn… they are programmed to learn… to find out, to want to know more. They are exploring and experiencing the world and it is our duty as adults to help them find the way to explore this wonderful world. I believe we must allow our children to taste the sweetness of their own knowledge and the knowledge they want to experience.

> "Real education consists in drawing the best out of yourself. What better book can there be than the book of humanity."
>
> **[Mahatma Gandhi]**

I believe our education system today is putting the cart before the horse. How is it that the child of two or three is eager to explore, eager to learn, eager to find out as much as they can? In fact, they are always researching through their interactions with the world, always looking for answers, always looking for new challenges. There is no need for anyone to force or push this process, it is natural and it happens with ease. Surely we must take heed of this and realise that when we interfere with the natural process the result is unhappy children being forced, bribed, pleaded with and begged to do their homework.

At school age, after a year at reception class, the child's natural desire to learn is being slowly taken from them. Why is this?

I believe it is because learning has now become a chore and it is often given in a way that is robotic, as the teacher has 30 children in a class and is trying to deal with many changing demands, and the simple fact that all children learn differently and need a different approach is lost.

It is simply not possible to focus on individual learning abilities in a class of 30 children where the major focus is preparation for tests. Not only is the teacher's own love of learning and teaching being lost, but the child has lost the spark to explore and has become programmed to sit exams.

I experienced this in all three schools my daughter attended. Her love for learning had become a chore and her excitement in wanting to learn something new slowly diminished.

> *"A child is not a vessel to be filled but a lamp to be lit."*
>
> **[Hebrew Proverb]**

As educators and parents we have a duty to help our children draw the best out of themselves, but before we can do this we must begin with ourselves.

And so armed with this knowledge I knew I had to continue to look at myself in order to understand how best to help my daughter grow into the beautiful woman she was to be.

The Adult: Obstacle or Support? (Had I become an obstacle in my daughter's Aspergers?)

Had I become an obstacle in my daughter's Aspergers? Yes, I realised that in my need to control everything I had in fact become an obstacle to my daughter's development. I was getting in her way and trying to get her to perform according to the plan in my head. I was so lost in my plan for her that I could not see the God-given plan she came with. So the next question came to me... what was my role in understanding the condition we were dealing with?

Children encounter many different adults in their daily life – from mum and dad to teachers and people in general. Each of us plays a role in the life of the child, where the child is a very keen observer in all the roles we play. The child watches everything we do and everything we are, resulting in the child learning more from our example than from our advice. The roles we play are a very important aspect of the child's life. Yet we often get lost in the roles we play and as a result become oblivious to the effect we have on the child.

Children are very aware and can see through all the parts we play in life, from the way we are with a stranger to our relationships with our loved ones. I knew I had to look at this because at an inner level I knew that I was often reacting to my daughter from a place of fear not love.

It's ironic that we are often politer to strangers, while to our loved ones and especially our children, we seem to turn into horror story versions of ourselves.

I became very aware of my actions and words after the following poem once again dropped into my inbox. It was a real eye-opener for me and a major wake-up call.

What Family Really Means:

I ran into a stranger as he passed by,
Oh, excuse me, please was my reply.
He said, "Please excuse me too;
I wasn't watching out for you."
We were very polite this stranger and I.
We went on our way and we said goodbye.
But at home a different story is told, how we treat our loved
ones young and old.

Later that day, cooking the evening meal, my daughter stood
beside me very still.
When I turned, I nearly knocked her down.
"Move out of the way," I said with a frown.
She walked away, her little heart broken.
I did not realise how harshly I'd spoken.

Later that night while I lay awake in bed God's voice came to me and said:

"While dealing with a stranger, common courtesy you use,
but with the children you love you seem to abuse.
Go and look on the kitchen floor, you will find some flowers behind the door.

Those are the flowers she brought for you.
She picked them herself: pink, yellow and blue.
She stood very quietly not to spoil the surprise.
And you never saw the tears that filled her little eyes."

By this time, I felt very small and now my tears began to fall.
I quietly went and knelt by her bed.
"Wake up, little one, wake up," I said.
"Are these the flowers you picked for me?"
She smiled, "I found them outside by the big tree.
I picked them because they are pretty like you.
I knew you'd like them especially the blue."
I said, "Oh, my darling I am so sorry for the way I acted today,
I shouldn't have yelled at you that way."
She said, "Oh mom, that's okay. I love you anyway."
I said; "My darling, I love you too and I do like the flowers, especially the blue."

[Unknown]

Are you aware that if we died tomorrow, the company that we are working for could easily replace us in a matter of days? But the family left behind will feel the loss for the rest of their lives. And come to think of it, we pour ourselves more into work than to our own family.

An unwise investment indeed.

FIND THE BALANCE

This poem was to cause me to travel on to the next leg of my journey. I had bought into the conditioned thinking that as adults we believe we are the guides and control the child's development. Yes, it is true that we are guides attempting to show the child the way through life, in the hope that they will develop naturally. But what we often miss is that the child is a more accurate guide to their own development and all we need to do is observe more than we instruct. In other words, we need to get out of the way and allow the child's natural development to unfold, while at the same time becoming a careful observer knowing when to step in and when to step back.

As a Montessori practitioner I learnt that I had to reflect on the impact I had on the developing child and my part in making a positive difference to the child. Often as practitioners we become unaware of how we are doing things; things become habitual – the way we respond to children, the constant instructing of children, not really listening to what they have to say, responding without truly understanding. This is not a judgement of how we do our work, rather a realisation that we fall into routines, habits and ways of doing things that stop us from seeing the effect we have on the developing child.

> *"We are not responsible for what our children do but we are responsible for how we respond to them."*
>
> **[Unknown]**

The problem lies in the fact that often our responses come from a place of lack and insecurity in ourselves, which in turn affects our responses. In many cases our responses are not enhancing the child's development but hindering it.

In turn we become obstacles to the child's development and as a result restrict his natural development.

Dr Montessori believed:

> *"That with proper care and help the child has it in him to grow to greater strength to attain a better mental balance and a more energetic character. Instead of leaving everything to chance the child's growth at this time should be a matter for scientific care and attention. This means that something more is needed than mere physical hygiene. Just as the latter wards off injuries to his body so we need mental hygiene to protect his mind and soul from harm."*
>
> **[M. Montessori, The Absorbent Mind page 13, 1948]**

The proper care and help is not only the responsibility of parents but also of teachers. I believe we must begin to think in terms of the child's mental and emotional development as being of paramount importance to his future and thus the future of our world. A great deal of time and money is spent on getting the academic curriculum right, with little emphasis on the emotional and mental development of the child. This seems to me to be putting the cart before the horse, as getting the child's mental and emotional balance right must surely be the main priority and when that is right the rest will automatically follow.

Dr Montessori believed this to be true 100 years ago, yet here we are 100 years later still focussing on getting the academics right while allowing the child's total development to lag behind.

It is my belief that we must begin to look at what *proper care and help* looks like.

However, before we can achieve this, I believe that we must begin with the adult and look at the changes we need to make to help in assisting the holistic development of the child.

It is not only the responsibility of the parent, but also of all practitioners who have given the time and commitment to become teachers, to take the next steps on the road to self-development and become reflective adults.

Be the Change You Want to See

"Be the change you want to see in the world."
Mahatma Gandhi

And as with my entire journey on this wonderful road, I once again found myself on the slip road to learning about reflection. I knew I had to change; I had done it my way for so many years trying to control everything, always looking for perfection, never being satisfied with what I did, full of expectations and always searching for the best way, totally oblivious to the fact that all the answers were before me in all the situations I found myself in every day.

I knew I had to step back and take stock and look at where I was in my life and how I had got here. In other words, reflect; but how was I going to do this?

I knew I had to look at this, as reflection had come up for me in so many ways and over many years of searching.

I thought it was for me to show others how to reflect on their work as my work with adults had dictated this, but as with every leg of my journey, I finally realised that this was my next lesson... I had to do it first.

My initial reaction was to set a schedule and add it to my list of things to do. Once again I found myself taking control and found myself pondering the possibility that this would be a wasted exercise. However, once I started to look at myself I soon realised that there was a great need to understand the importance of reflection, both personally and professionally.

Here I was, a Montessori teacher of 30 years, the mother of a child with Asperger syndrome and a traveller on a road of self-discovery that has so many potholes. I was lost in the confusion of not knowing myself, not knowing Aspergers and certainly not knowing where I was going.

Once again I was to return to my Montessori training and began to realise that, although I had trained 30 years ago, it was only through this amazing soul-searching journey that I'd begun to truly understand the transformative genius of the Montessori method.

Montessori advocated that the best preparation for teaching begins with a study of oneself.

She believed that an in-depth study of our values,

beliefs, habits, reactions, shortcomings and strengths was a most valuable tool in the preparation of working with young children.

She believed that in order to protect the child in all his innocence and vulnerability we, as educators, must begin with ourselves in order to determine how our personal characteristics inhibit or enhance our relationship with the child.

With this in mind I set out to become just that, although I was mindful of not falling into the trap of reflection becoming merely a technical tool; I wanted to transform and change.

> *"We insist that a teacher must prepare herself interiorly by systematically studying herself so that she can tear out her most deeply rooted defects those in fact which impede her relations with children. In order to discover these subconscious failings, we have need of a special kind of instruction. We must see ourselves as another sees us. We must be willing to accept guidance if we wish to become effective teachers"*
>
> **[A. Wolf, Nurturing the Spirit page 34, 1996]**

I was aware that reflection was needed both as a mother and a practitioner and I knew I had to begin to look at and reflect on my interactions with my own child.

And so I began to look at myself and evaluate my interactions and reactions and the possible triggers that caused my daughter's behaviours and meltdowns. I began by asking myself:

- What was causing her outbursts?

- What am I not seeing?
- How can I help?
- Am I in her way?
- Am I adding to the confusion?
- What is my agenda?
- Am I trying to prove a point?
- Why do I need to be in control?

The answer in many cases directed me to evaluate my responses and from this I realised that yes, in many instances the way I responded or dealt with a situation was the trigger for a meltdown.

This in turn led me on the road of self-discovery... a road travelled with some reluctance because I was now having to face the part of me that I hide from the world, the part that I hide from myself, the part that has been wounded. I knew I had to begin with this because it was in this part of me that I would find my true self and begin to awaken to the truth of who I really am.

As Dr Montessori once said:

> *"Fraternity is born more easily on the road of error than that of perfection."*

I knew from all the books I had read that to fully appreciate the art of reflection and self-discovery I must be willing to look at myself in a way that would allow the wounds to be exposed, while at the same time not be afraid to take a leap into the unknown; the place that would allow my true nature and character to be exposed. I was ready to take this leap as I knew that I had lived my life in the prison of my insecurities and fears and the time had come to make a difference so that I could support my precious little girl in being the amazing person she is.

Once I realised that this exposure was safe and a place where I could begin to heal the wounds and see myself in a light I never thought possible, my journey of reflection became more than a tool, it became a way of living.

> *"They say the best men are moulded out of faults, and, for the most, become much more the better for being a little bad."*
>
> **[William Shakespeare]**

I knew at this point that there was no turning back; I had lived my life in denial for years, accepting my reactions as normal, completely oblivious to the fact that I had a role to play in making the world a better place for our children, but I had to begin with my own child. I saw myself as an individual going about my life in a way that pleased me... but the irony of it was that it did not please me. I was simply living out a script that I had written for myself years ago. I had written a rather sad story and was simply playing a role in my own production.

I remembered reading once that Chief Seattle, the chief of the Suquamish, spoke of life as a web and that we are all connected. Humankind, he said:

> *...has not woven the web of life; we are but one thread within it. Whatever we do to the web we do to ourselves. All things are bound together. All things are connected. Man does not weave this web of life. He is merely a strand of it. Whatever he does to the web he does to himself."*

On reading this I had come to a profound realisation... my interactions and reactions were not only affecting my daughter they were also affecting me. I was getting more lost in the prison of my own fears and not only was I causing my daughter unnecessary anxieties, I was pushing myself deeper and deeper into the internal prison of my own making.

I had to get out – I had to break free. I was living in an age of advancement where we could communicate across the world in seconds, yet here I was in 2015 unable to communicate with my daughter. How had this happened? What had I missed? And then it happened... I realised that I did not know myself. I was simply a programme living in a programmed world, having allowed myself to be conditioned by society and the power of others. When had this happened, when had I lost my freedom?

Yet here I was doing exactly the same to my daughter; I was imprisoning her in my expectations and the expectations of the world.

I was indirectly teaching her how to be in the prison of not only my expectations, but the expectations of society. When did this happen? When did I stop living? When did I need the approval of others? The irony of all this was that I had not realised I had stopped living; my existence had become living to me. And here I was teaching my daughter the same things. Through fears and expectations, I was indirectly teaching her how not to trust her instinct, but to rely on the opinions of others.

I was teaching her that her happiness depended on

others and what they thought was good for her. Why had this happened? When had I stopped hearing myself? When had I stopped listening to my soul? How had unhappiness become a way of life for me and why was I teaching this to my precious daughter?

Funny thing is that I had not realised that I was accepting unhappiness as a way of life, but it was something that had somehow become a habit.

In fact, if truth be told, unhappiness seems to have become an epidemic, something that we feed our children every day in the way we live our lives.

Children of today are slowly being fed that they are not enough, if they don't get a good grade they are somehow failures, that they need something to make them happy, that happiness can only be found in things.

In a world with high-tech everything, the ability to cure the world of greed, hatred, unhappiness and pain has still not been found. Why is this? Why is it that we have progressed to talking to each other on the other side of the world while seeing each other on a screen, but we cannot be open with ourselves and see the truth of who we are?

It has become natural to accept all the sadness and pain we see in the world today and simply shrug it off with, "That's life". This is not life – life is gift; it is amazing, wonderful, a joy and a privilege. So why are we teaching our children to see life as anything other than the marvel it is?

A. S. Neill in his book *Summerhill* sums it up beautifully when he said:

> "All you need to allow happy children is the belief that children are good not bad and are innately wise and realistic."
> He believed that all crimes, all hatred, all wars can be reduced to unhappiness. "The difficult child is the child who is unhappy. He is at war with himself; and in consequence he is at war with the world. The difficult adult is the same. No happy man ever disturbed a meeting or preached war. No happy woman ever nagged her husband or her children. No happy man ever committed murder or theft. No happy employer ever frightened his employees. All crimes all hatred all wars can be reduced to unhappiness."
>
> **[A. S. Neill, Summerhill]**

We have to wake up to the fact that as adults we have a responsibility to show our children the marvel of this world and help them to see the beauty, not only in the world, but most importantly in themselves. This can only happen when reflection becomes part of the norm. This is especially important when working with children on the autistic spectrum. The marvel of the autistic child can only be revealed when they are understood and supported with understanding and love.

Aspergers and Education

Schools often miss the point when dealing with children with Aspergers. Firstly, I believe the problem lies in the fact that schools are oversubscribed and when faced with children with Aspergers they feel they have to 'deal' with them rather than see the child as s/he is; accepting where the child is rather than where they want the child to be.

Believe me, I am not blaming schools or teachers because there are many amazing and brilliant people in our schools today, but the problem lies with the simple fact that our schools are overcrowded and underfunded, so the teachers are trying to make the best of what they are given. This in turn affects the way children with Aspergers are taught in schools.

Teachers are given a certain amount of training where 'one size fits all' and all children with Aspergers are pretty much seen as the same, with the same issues. This in turn causes more confusion than clarity because children with Aspergers are all different; they learn, socialise, think, act, laugh and cry differently, all are unique just as every human being is on this amazing planet. We are made to take and give the best to this amazing world and to look for the best; yet we often fall into the trap of looking for the worst and seeing everything as a problem rather than an opportunity to learn.

We all have a purpose in this life and finding our purpose is the key to bliss. During the making of a documentary on autism my daughter said that people should see the character of the child before they see the autism… She said people must see their uniqueness first and then and only then can they be of any help to the child. How wonderful this is… seeing the child before the autism, because it is in seeing the child that true support can be given.

You Are Who You Are For A Reason

You are who you are for a reason
You're part of an intricate plan.
You're a precious and perfect unique design
Called God's special woman or man
You look like you look for a reason
Because God made no mistake
He knit you together within the womb
You're just what he wanted to make
The parents you have are the ones He chose
And no matter how you may feel
They are custom designed with God's plan in mind
And bear the Master's seal
You are who you are for a reason
You've been formed by the Master's rod
You are who you are beloved
Because there is a God.

[Russell Kelfer]

We are who we are for a reason and that's it in a nutshell. Labels and conditions are given to try to make sense of what looks unusual to the norm. I understand the thinking behind the labels, but I can also see the danger that pigeonholing labels can do. A dear friend once said to me about my precious daughter, "*Her soul does not have Aspergers or epilepsy.*"

This was a profound moment for me because at that moment I felt a sense of relief, because I could see beyond the Aspergers to the clarity and perfection of my daughter as the beautiful soul she is.

The Aspergers label had somehow put a barrier between me and my daughter because I saw everything she did as the fact that she had Aspergers and began to look out for the signs of Aspergers, rather than see my daughter for all she is. By reaching this place in myself I was able to separate the symptoms of Aspergers from the truth of my daughter. And so I was able to see that the way my daughter sees the world and the way she does and says certain things may be viewed by others as Aspergers, but on the whole her view of the world and her understanding of people and life are much deeper and more profound than I could imagine.

She allowed me to awaken to certain truths that lay dormant for years.

Because of her honesty and sincerity, I was able to be true to myself and question how I saw my own truth.

She has an innate spirituality that allows her to see things others have become closed to and for this I am truly grateful because she will always be true to herself and not try to conform to what others expect her to be. And this was one of the biggest problems I faced with schools. On the one hand she wanted to be in school and mix with other children while becoming fully immersed in her love of learning. But on every occasion the way she sees the world always got in the way and was so misunderstood.

Her Aspergers was seen as something that needed to be dealt with and moulded, where she needed to learn the way of the world rather than be true to herself and her way of seeing the world. Ironically I realised that his was also how I saw it, as I was trying to fix her and get her to see things the way I see them. On many occasions when we were in the middle of a difficult meltdown she would say, "I wish you could be in my body and know how it feels."

And this led me to my next lesson. I knew I had to learn about the condition my daughter was diagnosed with. I had to become versed in Aspergers... and so the next stage of my learning began...

So what exactly is Asperger syndrome? The NAS (National Autistic Society) says that Asperger syndrome is defined as the following:

"As soon as we meet a person we make judgements about them. From their facial expression, tone of voice and body language we can usually tell whether they are happy, angry or sad and respond accordingly. People with Asperger syndrome can find it harder to read the signals that most of us take for granted. This means they find it more difficult to communicate and interact with others which can lead to high levels of anxiety and confusion. Aspergers syndrome is a form of autism, which is a lifelong disability that affects how a person makes sense of the world, processes information and relates to other

Being a 'hidden disability' makes it much more difficult for children with Aspergers in all environments, from home to school to socialising in general. While they are trying to make sense of social situations that we take for granted, they are often left with an overwhelming feeling of loss, because not only are they misunderstood, but in many cases they are either blamed or judged for their inappropriate responses – something Yasmin and I deal with on a daily basis.

I could never understand how to view my daughter's inappropriate responses until I began to learn that they are simply a result of wanting to 'fit in' and trying to like everyone else, but not understanding or being able to read the situation.

This can be so debilitating because not only does she not understand the correct social responses, she is then being blamed or judged for getting it wrong – something she cannot control.

This is very obvious in school environments; on the one hand the child with Aspergers seems to understand the roles and routines of the school environment and tries to fit in to what is expected while at the same time trying to make sense of the things that seem totally alien to them. This in turn leads to teachers thinking that all is well when in fact the anxieties and confusions are hidden and internalised.

I had first-hand experience of this when my daughter went to high school. She was very eager to try high school as she had a desire to be with children her own age and to learn to socialise in an environment that she was unsure of.

However, after a period of time it became apparent that her desire to fit in and her need to learn to socialise were overpowered by how she makes *"sense of the world, processes information and relates to other people"*. Many things did not make sense to her, especially around social interactions. For example, the fact that teachers were so outwardly affected when she asked certain questions that to her were logical. For example where a teacher originated from, as my daughter's love of geography made her curious about places of origin. It made little sense to my daughter when the teachers would see this question as rude.

And to be perfectly honest, I too find it a bit strange that someone could see this question as rude! (Perhaps I have Aspergers!)

However, this showed clearly as a classic example of how the teacher in this case did not take the time to reflect on how her response could cause my daughter, or any child, unnecessary anxiety and confusion. In my daughter's mind (and in mine too) this was a very logical question and one that a person should not take offence to.

This incident prompted me to look further into the responses of teachers and the effect they have on a child with Aspergers, with specific reference to social communication and social interaction; both something we take for granted but for a child with Aspergers something that can cause a great deal of anxiety and fear.

I have observed my daughter in many such situations, where she tries to read the social interactions taking place and desperately wants to join in but does not know the appropriate response, only to end in an inappropriate response which results in the people around her judging her or blaming her for her behaviour or response.

As a mother it hurts my heart to watch this play out, as I just want to jump in and help her not to look or act so socially awkward. I have watched her try so hard to know how to respond to situations, only to be left more anxious as her response was not the 'correct' one. This often happens in Ireland, as being half Irish and spending a lot of time in Ireland she tries to fit into the Irish way. Now anyone who has experienced a typical Irish family situation with lots of banter, jokes and ten conversations going on at one time, knows that you most certainly need to understand the rules of socialising.

This is something she finds so difficult and on many occasions she has been totally lost, which ends with her leaving the room to be by herself where she can feel safe. On these occasions I try to role play what took place and show her how she could respond, which she fully understands and is happy about until she tries to use my advice in another similar situation only for it to be the wrong response, which once again leads to blame and judgement, leaving her feeling totally insecure and unsure of her own understanding.

The difficulty, I believe, lies in the fact that people don't understand the condition and are simply responding to her from a place of familiarity, from their own social awareness and understanding, which is not very helpful to my daughter's social understanding.

Gunilla Gerland explains this very clearly in her book, *A Real Person* (1997), when she talks about how her parents could not understand her differences and difficulties in interacting with her family and friends. Firstly, she said the difficulty lay in the fact that she was not diagnosed until she was in her twenties and secondly her parents...

> "...*measured her according to the way they measured themselves.*" This in turn left her feeling a deep sense of failure and confusion... "*I was miserable inside because they thought me spoilt and lazy, and I thought they were right.*"
>
> **[G. Gerland, A Real Person]**

When I read Gerland's book it was an awakening moment for me. I realised that I too measured Yasmin according to the way I measured myself, which led to me having very high expectations of her, leaving little room in my head for her uniqueness and differences. This in turn leads to many problems, from low self-esteem to a lack of confidence, which in turn forces the person to either withdraw completely from all social interactions or spend their life trying to please others so that they will be accepted by so-called 'normal people' into what they are led to believe is 'normal society'.

This is something I believe my daughter struggled

with, however I now realise that it is not only her struggle, but something that I struggle with in my quest to help her to 'fit in' to so-called 'normal society'. I realise that I had become so conditioned to what 'normal' should look like that I had lost my truth of 'unique'.

My daughter is unique and perfect in every way, thank God, and it is my limitations and fears that are stopping me from seeing who she is.

I realised, with some sadness, that my energies are spent on looking for ways to help her 'fit in' to normal societal expectations and in so doing I am blinded to the fact that she is very capable and aware of being a part of the society she lives in. She herself does not have a need to fulfil societal expectations because she loves the way she sees the world and is happy to see the world as she does.

I realised that it is my desire for 'normal' that causes certain anxieties and so with this realisation I continued my search for answers to the condition of Aspergers so that I could understand the condition that had become our way of life.

My search landed me on the road of the overwhelming concept of social communication. Wow! That was a big one. Here I was at the age of 50, having learned how to communicate socially from my Irish family upbringing, looking for ways to help my child make sense of all this.

Understanding Social Communication in a World of Confusion

And so once again I turned to the NAS in search of more information and fell on their explanation of social communication. They suggest that understanding social communication to a person with Aspergers is like trying to understand a foreign language, as someone with Aspergers finds it difficult to express themselves emotionally and socially, which results in difficulties in understanding gestures, facial expressions and tone of voice, or simply how to start a conversation.

Now for the daughter of an Irish mother this was even more difficult, because as Irish people we can't help but talk with our hands and expressions, and our tone of voice is certainly something you would need lessons in to understand.

Friends who have visited my home in Ireland and do not have Aspergers ask me to translate! So for my darling daughter her lack of social communication understanding is something she certainly struggles with when she is in Ireland. On many occasions I am caught between wanting to laugh at the funny things she says and cry because she does not realise that she is being funny.

The ironic thing was that when I first encountered Yasmin in this situation I merely thought she was shy, something I suffered from as a child, so I presumed it was just inherited and it was something she would grow out of. That of course was until I saw her in other social situations where she was a lot more confident and in fact seemed very comfortable. She expressed herself in a very mature way and seemed to be very aware of the people around her and was often seen as very mature and confident. Seeing her in these situations gave me a clue as to why the adults around her responded to her in a negative and frustrated way, something I do on occasion, as my expectations of her are that she should know how to behave. This causes so much anxiety for her, as on the one hand she is trying to make sense of something she does not understand, while on the other hand she is trying to please me.

People see her as mature and she is also tall for her age so looks older, which results in people having an expectation based on their own understanding and perceptions of how she should behave in a certain way and when she does something that they perceive as rude or inappropriate, they react in a negative and frustrated manner.

This in turn leads to more inappropriate behaviours and comments, because now Yasmin is totally unaware of what is happening so resorts to what she understands within herself and this is due to the high levels of anxiety she feels, which she is unable to resolve. She will often laugh or say something out of context, which will lead to all manner of negative responses from people around her and from me.

The problem, I believe, is that we have a certain idea of what social communication looks like based on our own experiences and perceptions. For example, you meet someone for the first time and you offer them your hand to greet them. In some cultures this is not done and so you take your hand back and know that the person does not shake hands. There is no confusion because you may have experienced this before or you read the body language and know by reading the situation what you should do next.

For the person with Aspergers it is not so clear cut and matter of fact... because the anxieties begin from the moment they are going to meet the person. A whole range of sensory issues become something to consider and on top of that they may have learnt that shaking hands is the way to greet someone, something they do not want to do anyhow, because touch is something they feel uncomfortable with but something they have learnt to deal with. But now the rules have changed because this person does not shake hands. Wow! What to do? The confusion has now added to the anxieties of greeting the person where the unwritten social rules are not understood.

How confusing must this be for a child with Aspergers, because for us we can read the situation almost before it happens, by reading body language and facial expressions, so we are prepared if there is a sudden change in social etiquettes. But for the child with Aspergers it adds to their confusion because they cannot read the situation, body language or facial expressions and have nothing to base their next move on... a difficult game and an exhausting feat.

I realised early into Yasmin's diagnosis that she found social communication very difficult. I was then faced with a dilemma; on the one hand I wanted to force her into social situations, while at the same time protect her from the anxieties that were brought up as a result of social interactions. It was then I found myself becoming very anxious in her social awkwardness and would literally push her into social situations that I could see were causing her so much pain and anxiety. I knew this was wrong and therefore I had to reflect on why I was doing this and realised it was for me, as I was uncomfortable and at times embarrassed by her social awkwardness.

This all came back to my own childhood and the expectations on us as children to be polite and speak when you are spoken to. It was unheard of that you would ignore someone who was speaking to you and greeting someone who greeted you was a must. And if you didn't greet them politely you got the 'look' that told you you were 'in for it' later! So from an early age we learnt how to be polite and no matter whether you were shy or you did not like the person, you learnt to 'pretend' and greet them in a way that had your mammy filled with pride at the great little girl you had become. We became great little actors and knew how to get the look of pride on our mammy's face!

This realisation was to become my next clue in this difficult journey of Aspergers. Yasmin could not act or pretend in social situations. She could work only from a place of 'what is', from 'logic' and asking her to try and interact, even if she did not want to or even if it caused her a certain amount of stress, seemed crazy to her.

She would ask me, "Why should I pretend or lie if I don't feel comfortable in a situation?" I knew she was right, as I was bringing her up to be true to herself and to be who she is, not someone she is expected to be. Once again I was faced with an issue that I didn't know how to explain.

I knew she was correct but I also had to try to teach her about the other side of socialising. This brought up so much for me because I had to reflect on the fact that in some social situations we are in fact pretending or lying, because if we were to say how we really feel we would hurt someone's feelings.

For my daughter however, hurting someone's feelings by telling them the truth seemed stranger. I was faced with questions like, "Why is being honest with someone something they should have a problem with?" This in turn led to many discussions around the immaturity of other people and the fact that some people are not ready for the truth, so we have to imagine how telling them the truth of how you feel would make them feel. Once again my daughter had become a mirror for me because she also spoke truths about how I would deal with certain situations and this led to me not wanting to face the truth of how she saw me. This brought me right back to what Dr Montessori said about changing yourself, by seeing yourself as others see you.

Not only does she force me to look at myself from her perspective, she also allows me to see how it must be for her. It was difficult for me to understand how she could not see things from another perspective until I saw her in situations where we would have major conflicts; then I could see by the strengths of her reactions to me that she was unable to see what I was trying to say. That was until she had calmed down and she could begin to make sense of it from another level.

This led to my understanding Aspergers a little more, as people with Aspergers find it difficult to put themselves in the shoes of other people. When I first explained this to Yasmin she was appalled that I would want her to wear another 'person's shoes' (taken literally). Although I understood this fact about Aspergers I still could not understand why my little girl found socialising such a major issue, as it came so naturally to me. On the one hand I realised that it did not come naturally to her and I was aware of the limitations of Aspergers, but in some situations she expressed herself very confidently. However, in others she would become withdrawn and seem uninterested in other people, appearing almost aloof and behaving in what may seem an inappropriate and rude manner.

As a mother this was something that was very difficult to observe. When I would take Yasmin to places with other children it would quickly become obvious that she found social interactions very difficult and confusing.

It was as if she did not know what to do. Her difficulty manifested itself in her inability to initiate conversation and know how to approach children. She found it very difficult to approach children and her levels of anxiety were so obvious.

Children would approach her but she would not know what to do; on many occasions I found myself speaking for her and asking her to tell the other child who she was etc. This always ended in the other child moving on, as they could see that Yasmin would not continue talking and would resort to shaking her piece of paper to reduce her anxieties. As a result, I would leave social situations and when friends invited me to parties I would decline as I knew that Yasmin's anxiety levels would be too much for her to bear.

As I home educate Yasmin it was easy for me to protect her from social situations, but it soon became clear to me that I needed to move her in a new direction and therefore put her in situations where she would feel anxious while at the same time protected. I was aware that speaking for her and protecting her from social situations was handicapping her and as a result felt I needed to do something not to handicap her.

"Don't handicap your children by making their lives easy."

[Robert A. Heinlein]

I knew I had to stop handicapping her by trying to protect her from her fear of interacting and take a leap into the world of social confusion. And so the home education groups became a new source of anxiety for us.

I remember the first time I took her to a home education group. Boy oh boy, what a painful experience! I could feel her tension rising the moment we stepped inside the hall. She gave me the look which said: GET ME

OUT OF HERE... I believed I had to persist and allow her to feel the tension and anxiety that was so apparent in her body language, while at the same time be sure she felt safe. She was in pain and this was breaking my heart. My immediate reaction was to put my arms around her, wrap her up in my warmth and the smell of my perfume (which she loves) and tell her everything would be alright and let's go. But I had been here before and I had done just that, resulting in her staying in the same place socially and that was something I knew I had to stop.

And so we persisted and I would not leave places until she made contact with one child in the place. As she tends to have a strong will (something I am sure she gets from her Irish roots!) I knew she would do it because she knew I would not leave until she'd made contact. So she would force herself to walk over to where the other children were and try to initiate conversations. It was at these moments that I knew we were beginning a new phase of our journey down the 'yellow brick Aspergers road'. I thought we had a breakthrough, albeit one that resulted in being told, "I did it now let's get out of here."

This was the beginning of a new direction on our road of social understanding; a road we travel every day with a lot of potholes and dead ends, yet a road so many parents take for granted. Yet for my daughter, and many children like her, social interactions can feel like a minefield, with every step becoming a possible threat to her safety.

This is something many people find hard to understand as they cannot put themselves in the shoes of a child with Aspergers, just like the child with Aspergers is unable to put themselves in the shoes of a person without Aspergers.

As much as I was learning about Aspergers and beginning to understand certain aspects of this condition, I was still baffled as to what could cause Yasmin such high levels of anxiety when faced with certain social situations. On the one hand I knew about the limitations of Aspergers, but it had to be more than that because of the fact that she could socialise very well in certain situations. I knew it had to be something to do with the different situations, but what was it about these situations that at one level allowed her to socialise with confidence and at another level send her into high levels of anxiety?

And then the answers came in a most unusual encounter. I happened upon a website called 'Aspergers Experts'. I had found many Aspergers websites before and read endless accounts of Aspergers, but this one was different as it was led by two young men who lived every day with Aspergers. They had first-hand experience of living with Aspergers and could tell it as it is. On listening to one of their web videos the penny dropped; it was a light bulb moment.

The thing that struck me most was when they explained that you cannot push a child with Aspergers into social situations because it is not the socialising that's the problem, it is the sensory issues relating to the social situation.

Here I was forcing Yasmin into social situations that she was unable to do, as she was focussing on the sensory issues of sounds, smells and touch that were sending her into social meltdowns. It became so clear to me and so I began to look at the situations we were going into and together we began to look at the possible sensory triggers

– from smells to sounds, to the energy Yasmin was picking up from the people around her.

This opened a new door for us because it allowed Yasmin to be back in the driving seat. I'd become intoxicated by the endless barrage of 'she must socialise', 'she's home educated, what about socialising?', 'what about mixing with other children?', I was overwhelmed by so many questions and comments about socialising and I was buying into all this pressure from other people believing that I must force her to mix even if it caused her so much pain and trauma.

What was I thinking?

Had I got so lost in the expectations of others that I was asleep to what was really needed? My daughter does know how to socialise and understands the different aspects to social interactions, which I could see in certain social situations that she felt comfortable in. The issues arose when there was sensory overload, where there were too many sensory issues to deal with. I began to see it as similar to a person who cannot swim; you would not throw them into the deep end and tell them to swim. And so I knew I had to stop throwing my daughter into the deep end and expecting her to socialise as I would. We had to take this slowly and allow her to feel her way in her social understanding and this could only happen by trying to minimise the sensory issues surrounding the places we would go.

Letting Go Was the Only Way Forward

And so the next answer came to me... I had reached a point where 'letting go' was the only way forward. Letting go of what I believed was 'normal'. Letting go of my preconceived ideas of how she should behave, how she should look to the world. Letting go of what people would say; what people would think. When I realised that I was concerned about what people would think then I knew I had to let go of my conditioned and rigid thinking. I found myself making excuses for my daughter – apologising for her ways, her behaviours – always sitting in company with my shoulders tensed afraid of what she may say or do (because she might offend someone).

So many times I would go to play areas only to be confronted by irate mothers who would be so insulted by my daughter's behaviour. She would often push other children out of her way, something I could not understand until now. I now know she was feeling sensory overload and needed to get away from the situations around her at whatever cost.

I remember when she was diagnosed a psychologist said that there are two types of Asperger character – fight or flight; one being a fighter and one a 'flighter'. My daughter is a fighter and will fight to get her point across or to get out of a situation that is hurting her, with no consideration for what is around her or no consideration for her own safety. At that moment she is in fight mode and she literally does not see what is around her. On so many occasions I was left with an overwhelming feeling of loss because I just did not know what to do when she was in this mode.

I did not understand and was unable to deal with this appropriately, as I was feeling lost and afraid and just wanted her to behave normally.

On one level I could understand how other mothers were feeling because their child had been pushed, but at the same time my need to protect my daughter was more important to me. Sadly, the mothers who would challenge my daughter could never see past their own perceptions of how a child should behave. Ironically this was something that I was also feeling, as I wanted my daughter to behave in an acceptable way. I was caught in an emotional tug of war between my love and desire to protect my daughter and my own personal need to see her as 'normal'. I found myself in so many situations where I just wanted her to adapt to the way that was acceptable, as I was brought up to always understand the unwritten rules of acceptable and appropriate behaviour and I wanted her to be the same.

It was not until a particular day in a play area when my daughter once again pushed a child out of her way that I began to question my attitude and look at things differently.

I was sitting trying to have a quiet, relaxed coffee (a very rare treat because my senses are always heightened!) when I saw a woman approach my daughter and begin to lecture her. Now bearing in mind my daughter was eight years old at this stage, I was shocked to see this outburst from the parent.

Once I was aware what was happening (relaxed coffee discarded!) I went to the woman and told her to come to me and not challenge my daughter, as I would have come to her should the situation be reversed (common courtesy I thought and an adult should never approach another child).

The woman was not very polite about things so I decided to approach the situation with calm and peace (although I was not feeling very calm at the time).

However, I decided to sit with the woman and explain to her that my daughter had Aspergers and that she did not mean to push her child, not for the reasons she thought, rather it was because she was overloaded with sensory stimuli. Her response sent a shiver down my spine and my Irish roots took on an almost demonic hysteria that, had I not contained them, someone would have been hitting the floor and it would not have been me!

She looked at me and said, "I am sorry for you; it must be awful to have a child like that." Oh my Lord it took all my strength to walk away and not floor her.

I was shocked to think that another mother could even think such thoughts and see any child as 'a child like that'. What did she mean? How was she seeing this?

So many things went through my mind at that moment; so much so that once I had relaxed I began to reflect on what had happened.

I realised that I too was at some level feeling the difficulty of dealing with a child with Aspergers and I was focussing on her Aspergers more than her being a beautiful sweet child. I was so caught up in the behaviours of her Aspergers and her stemming that I was unable to see the truth of her spirit. The lesson was mine and showed me that it was 'me' who needed to change in order to accept and enjoy the beautiful gift I was given.

And so the journey continued in a new direction – the direction of 'letting go'.

Letting go of the conditioning, the controlled, preconceived ideas of my limited self and open to the truth and wonder of this amazing journey from confusion to clarity.

> *"You are what you love not what loves you."*
>
> **[Charlie Kaufman's film Adaptation]**

It was at this stage that so many things became clear to me. By letting go of the control I was freeing myself from my past and getting out of not only my own way, but more importantly, of my daughter's way. I was then able to see more clearly. It was also at this time that I finally understood what the psychologist was telling me at her diagnosis – "that I was adding to her anxiety". I realised that for so long I was lost in my need to control everything – from my life to my daughter's Aspergers.

I thought that if I could control her Aspergers that she would somehow act 'normal' and I would not have to deal with her unusual behaviours, or more to the point, the attitudes and expectations of other people around her behaviours.

I had finally admitted to myself that I was out of control and here I was in 2015 realising that there was no way of controlling my daughter or the Aspergers. And there was no need to try to control the Aspergers.

> *It is simply as it is, it is our way of life, something I had to surrender to and allow to be, something to be honoured and loved, something to embrace with every limb, something to fully accept as it is.*
>
> **[Mags]**

As a result of this realisation things began to make more sense to me – to become clearer. Aspergers is our way of life, it is what we live every day, it is not only a condition, it is an amazing adventure.

It is our way of life, filled with laughter and tears, and I would not have it any other way. Acceptance of where we were allowed me to see what I needed to change in me.

Not only did I need to learn to let go, I also began to realise that I was often the catalyst in my daughter's outbursts.

My reactions and responses were a huge part of how she felt about herself and I saw that this in turn was leading to self-esteem and confidence issues. It became clear to me that how I dealt with her behaviours was a major factor in her development and I found that on occasion my reactions were like that of a child having a tantrum. And, as with every part of this amazing journey, I was once again sent a message. The following story mysteriously dropped into my inbox.

> One evening an old Cherokee told his grandson about a battle that goes on inside people. He said, "My son the battle is between two wolves inside us all.
>
> "One is evil; it is anger, envy, jealously, sorrow, regret, greed, arrogance, self-pity, guilt, resentment, inferiority, lies, false pride, superiority and ego.
>
> "The other is good. It is joy, peace, love, hope, serenity, humility, kindness, benevolence, empathy, generosity, truth, compassion and faith."
>
> The grandson thought about it for a moment and then asked his grandfather, "Which wolf wins?"
>
> The old Cherokee simply replied.
>
> **"The one you feed."**

And so I was once again faced with the need to reflect on which wolf I had become accustomed to feeding, and more importantly, how this was affecting my daughter. Was I adding to her confusion and anxiety, or was I giving her a safe place to find answers?

I knew I had to be honest with myself and on many occasions I realised that I was in fact adding to her confusion and pain, and was not always giving her a safe place to find answers because I did not know the answers.

I was looking in all the wrong places for answers, searching outside myself, because I too was afraid and was reacting from a place of fear. I knew I had to take responsibility for myself and look deep within to find the source of my fears so that I could be the safe place my daughter craved.

> *"The absence of fear is the finest thing that can happen to a child."*
>
> **[A. S. Neill, Summerhill]**

Finally Taking Responsibility for Me

It was at this stage that I realised that I was full of fear and anxiety, still holding on to the fears and pain of the past. The time had come to finally 'grow up' and take responsibility for me.

I had spent enough years lost in my own anxieties and the anxieties of others; still waiting for the moment when I would finally live in the freedom of not being afraid. I had to do this not only for myself, but more importantly, for Yasmin.

She deserved a mum who could respond to her in a mature and non-judgemental way. And so my journey continued in the knowledge that I had the power to change.

Rome wasn't built in a day… but it had to begin with the first brick and so I knew I had to find the first brick to begin the next stage of my journey.

But where was I to go now? I had tried so many different things. How was I going to take responsibility for me?

And then I got this message:

> *"One thing we do know; life will give you whatever experience is most helpful for the evolution of your consciousness. How do we know this is the experience you need? Because this is the experience you are having at this moment."*
>
> **[Eckhart Tolle]**

And so I began to become conscious; to awaken to the experiences I was having, knowing that life was offering me all the experiences I needed to evolve. And the experiences came in the most unusual ways and times.

Once I realised that life was sending me everything I required to evolve I began to awaken and become conscious of the moment, realising that the only moment that matters is 'now', the past is done and the 'now' is shaping our future. I had read so much about being present, about being in the now. But I found it so difficult to understand how I was not in the now – here I was living my life in the now; my day-to-day living was here and now, so how was I not experiencing the peace and freedom of the 'now'?

And then the penny dropped; once I became aware of the difference between my body being in the 'now' and my thoughts jumping in and out of the past and the future. I was then able to feel the meaning of being in the 'moment' – because I started to surrender to 'what is' and as a result became present with my whole being – not just my body.

And this became the next stage for me; becoming aware of being in the moment with my daughter and alive in that very moment, not second-guessing everything she is to become, or how she will cope when she is older. I simply became present with her and hear and see her in the moment, fully aware of what was happening in that moment, not judging it on a memory of the past or a fear of the future.

I began to awaken to what 'is' around me not what 'was' around me or what 'will be' around me in some distant future.

My unconscious 'zombie'-like state got a rude awakening. I began to feel the moment I was in – experiencing it with my whole being – self, soul and mind.

And so you may ask, what difference would this make to my relationship with my daughter? It makes an amazing difference; it brings truth to life in every moment of each experience we have together.

Things began to become clearer to me. When faced with, what I perceive as a difficult situation, I am now able to remain focussed in the moment – in what is happening and not draw on issues from the past or fears of the future. Although at times it is not as easy as it sounds and as much as I try to remain focussed and present, it does not happen all the time. At times, my daughter would confidently tell you that I resort back to my conditioned and frightened state, which results in negative reactions and blame; but thank God they are becoming much less frequent.

Saying that, and not judging myself for my relapses, it has become very clear to me that when I do remain focussed and aware of the situation before us both with no drawing from the past or the future, situations are resolved very quickly and with a very positive and empowering outcome. Yasmin is left feeling safe, secure and empowered in the knowledge that her mum is being a mature, responsible adult and not resorting to childlike behaviour and tantrums, and I am left with a sense of peace and security.

I realised that it was only in the moments of conflict and confusion that I could really test my theory of staying focussed. And so I began to observe myself in the difficult situations:

- I do this by witnessing the drama that unfolds around us, but I do not become the drama.
- I do this by not letting the drama manipulate and control me.

As soon as I allow my conditioned self, full of preconceived ideas and expectations, to take over, I am unable to respond with clarity and instead react from a place of fear, which ultimately results in the situation getting out of control.

For any child this is a very difficult and scary place to be – but for a child with Aspergers it takes on a totally different meaning and sends them into meltdown, because they have no mechanism to make sense of something that to them makes absolutely no sense.

And so equipped with this understanding I began to focus on staying present in a difficult situation and seeing it for what it was, rather than for what my perception of it was.

The Power of Love

> "When you choose to put love into what you do the universe will move heaven and earth to let you do what you love."
>
> **[Abraham-Hicks]**

And so my journey continued with my beautiful daughter trying to make sense of a world she saw so differently, while at the same time trying to make sense of my reactions. By now I had come to realise that my negative reactions came from a place of fear not love. I knew deep inside me that the absence of fear is the finest thing that can happen to a child.

However, I was so lost in my own fears that I could not get past them, so I knew that I had to deal with the fears that I was carrying around with me and I had to find a way to change.

I always believed and lived by the belief that every child needs to know they are loved, regardless of behaviour. You have to be on the side of a child, no matter what. And I knew that you simply could not be on the side of a child if you punished and stormed at them with your own fears and insecurities.

> *"The greatest adventure a human being can undertake is the journey from the ego the 'I' to the self the divine consciousness that exists within each of us."*
>
> **[Shaykh F. Haeri]**

I knew I could not continue on the road of insecurity and fear, because not only was I living in my own self-made prison of fear and anxiety, my precious little girl was growing up and looking to me for clues to her development. I had to take stock and look at ways that I could change, but first I had to find ways of changing how I saw my life.

The problem at the time was that I was caught up in some annoying outer stuff and I was attached to all the chaos and drama around me looking for ways to improve my life. I was unaware at the time that all I needed was to trust in the process of life and allow the journey to unfold, while at the same time do whatever I had to. I had not realised that I had lost trust, as the drama and chaos of my life had sent me into a tornado of emotions, which kept me stuck in the problem. I knew I had to find a way to trust again but the million-dollar question was 'how'?

I knew that life was giving me the experiences I needed and so I began to accept where I was as the place I needed to be... This was an awakening moment, as I had struggled for years to fight what I did not like and in the fight I was getting more stuck.

I knew that if I accepted where I was and the situations I found myself in, I would find a solution with fewer struggles. And therefore surrendering to what was before me became my mantra.

I had tried this before but never really got it, until I realised that I was causing unnecessary anxiety and fear for both me and Yasmin and no amount of positive talking or telling myself that this must stop was working; so the only thing left to do was to surrender... to let go... Not give up, but to surrender and accept exactly where we were in our journey through Aspergers and life. It was at this stage that I began to realise that life would give you exactly what you need once you are open to seeing it. And so I began to become open to what life was showing me. I began to accept that life was showing me the way and all I had to do was follow without judgements or fear of what would be.

It was in the acceptance of where we were that I was able to see what was really before me and that was my beautiful, talented, loving little girl who was full of love and life.

It was then that I was able to connect to the love that I felt for Yasmin, rather than to connect to the place of fear and control that I had become so accustomed to. I began to focus on what was beautiful about our relationship, about our life, and see the good in everything and every situation that came to us. I knew I had spent enough years wallowing in guilt and beating myself up for getting things wrong; from causing her Aspergers, to not understanding, to having postnatal depression, to extreme guilt... the list was endless. I knew this had to stop, this was not helping me and it was certainly not helping my precious little girl.

She needed me to stop... to stop beating myself up...

to stop wallowing in guilt... to stop being afraid of the future and how things would be for her. This was only bringing me down and as a result teaching her that 'fear is our way of life'.

Mahatma Gandhi said, "Be the change you want to see in the world." And so I became the change I wanted to see in our lives. It had to happen... the victim had to go. The past had no power over me unless I gave it power... the future had not yet come, so why worry about it? The best of everything was happening right here, right now.

And with this epiphany my relationship with my daughter could continue from a much healthier place... a place of love not fear. A place where I could finally begin to take responsibility for me and the example I was showing her in my reactions and behaviour. And so my daughter's Aspergers became our way of life, rather than her condition.

It was no longer something we had to 'deal' with. It was our way of life... amazing, happy and full of love; ironically something my daughter always knew, as it was second nature to her. She does not try to be someone else, she does not try to 'fit in', but she knew that my need to please was trying to make her be something else in order to 'fit in'.

I had been asleep to her amazing understanding of life and her genuine sense of self-worth, and because my sense of self-worth was compromised, I was pushing this on her in the guise of her needing to change.

I must have done something right though, as she is very confident in who she is. So the question I found myself asking myself was: why could I not do this for myself? I had given my daughter the tools to develop a strong belief in herself, yet where had my sense of self-worth gone?

The answer was simple – my self-belief was not gone, it was dormant and ready to emerge. And so this wonderful journey from confusion to clarity was not only helping me understand Aspergers syndrome in order help my daughter in her journey through this minefield, but it was also allowing me to unfold and realise my true purpose in life… being a mother to my amazing and funny daughter.

Awakening to the Truth

Asperger syndrome is not a defect – it is not a condition; it is a way of life. Autistic children are amazing; they are real in so many senses of the word. Their truth is profound and they have an exceptional ability to feel the world around them.

They should not be pushed to do things they are not ready to do. They should not be condemned for not understanding the ways of the world, they should not be made to feel insecure or afraid to be who they are.

They should be honoured for the truth of who they

are, supported to be the best of who they can be and seen as the amazing children they are.

In my confusion and expectations of my daughter's social understanding, I was trying to force her into situations she was not yet ready to try. I was desperate for her to be 'normal' and do things that other children could do easily. I was afraid that her difference and her lack of social awareness would become a problem in her life.

I realised in my need to get her to do things that I thought she should do, I was in fact fulfilling my own desire for 'normal', oblivious to what was best for her or what she needed at the time. And for this I am truly sorry my darling Yasmin.

A dear friend and teacher advised me that my daughter should not be forced to do anything that is not easy for her. More important is to accept her state and try to see where her deep subconscious lies. This was the best advice I could have received, as it allowed me to see where I had become the obstacle to my daughter's development and uniqueness.

It is my aim in writing this book to share this advice with anyone who will listen and ask that we accept the depth of our amazing children and allow them to be who they are and support them in whatever way we can to help them to be true to themselves.

I was once reminded that in previous days it was the given practice to make everyone like the 'norm', something I tried to do until I woke up. We must not force our children or try to make them 'normal'. We must allow their uniqueness to shine a torch for us to follow.

> *"It is so true that psychology and the social sciences traditionally tried to refit everyone into a mould – the cookie cutter syndrome I call it. But this actually doesn't work moreover it dishonours the individual gift of who we are."*
>
> **[Aliya B. Haeri, ASK]**

I now encourage my daughter to explore who she is and to find her interests, in order to allow her to connect with her true self. I urge all parents to encourage their children to be who they are and to be there for them when they have lost their way.

Our children need a life jacket when they are drowning in their anxieties and fears and we as parents need to be that for them.

Yasmin and I no longer look for the problem but look for the solution and it is in looking for the solution that everything becomes clear for us.

> *"If you intend to be of assistance, your eye is not upon the trouble but upon the assistance, and that is quite different. When you are looking for a solution, you are feeling positive emotion—but when you are looking at a problem, you are feeling negative emotion."*
>
> **[Abraham]**

It was with this understanding that the pieces of the puzzle starting falling into place. Thank God.

The End

Lightning Source UK Ltd.
Milton Keynes UK
UKOW07f0608270916

283908UK00011B/61/P